OTHER BOOKS IN THIS SERIES:

For a wonderful Mother A book to make your own
For a wonderful Grandmother A book to make your own
For a real Friend A book to make your own
A Girl's Journal A personal notebook and keepsake
A Woman's Journal A personal notebook and keepsake
Cats A book to make your own
Teddy Bears A book to make your own
Inspirations A book to make your own

OTHER HELEN EXLEY GIFTBOOKS
ON GARDENS:

Garden Quotations
The Crazy World of Gardening
The Littlest Gardening Giftbook

Published in hardback 1990 Published in softcover 2001.
Copyright © Helen Exley 1990, 2001
Selection © Helen Exley 1990, 2001
The moral right of the author has been asserted.

12 11 10 9 8 7 6 5 4

ISBN 1-86187-214-3

Selection and design by Helen Exley
Illustrated by Juliette Clarke
Printed in China
Dedicated to Richard, whose love of gardening makes my world astounding, peaceful, new every day – Helen.

Exley Publications Ltd, 16 Chalk Hill, Watford, Herts, WD19 4BG, UK.
Exley Publications LLC, 232 Madison Avenue, Suite 1409, NY 10016, USA.
www.helenexleygiftbooks.com
The publishers are grateful for permisson to reproduce copyright material. Whilst every reasonable effort has been made to trace copyright holders, we would be pleased to hear from any not here acknowledged. Reginald Arkell: "Those Latin Names" from *Green Fingers*. Used by permission of Barrie and Jenkins Ltd. Henry Beard and Roy McKie: From *Gardening: A Gardener's Dictionary* © 1982 Henry Beard and Roy McKie. Used by permission of Workman Publishing Inc. Robin Clarke: From *The Completely Unillustrated Encyclopaedia of Gardening*. This first appeared in New Scientist magazine London. Paul Jennings: From an article in The Observer, April 1962. Laurie Lee: From *Cider With Rosie*. Used by permission of Chatto and Windus Ltd. Sara Teasdale: From "Night". Used by permission of Macmillan Publishing Company from *Collected Poems of Sara Teasdale*' © 1930 Sara Teasdale Filsinger, renewed 1958 by Guaranty Trust Co. of New York. Alan Titchmarsh: From *The Gardener's Logbook*. Used by permission of William Collins Sons & Co Ltd and Lennard Publishing.

A Gardener's Journal

A BOOK TO MAKE YOUR OWN

A HELEN EXLEY GIFTBOOK

≣EXLEY

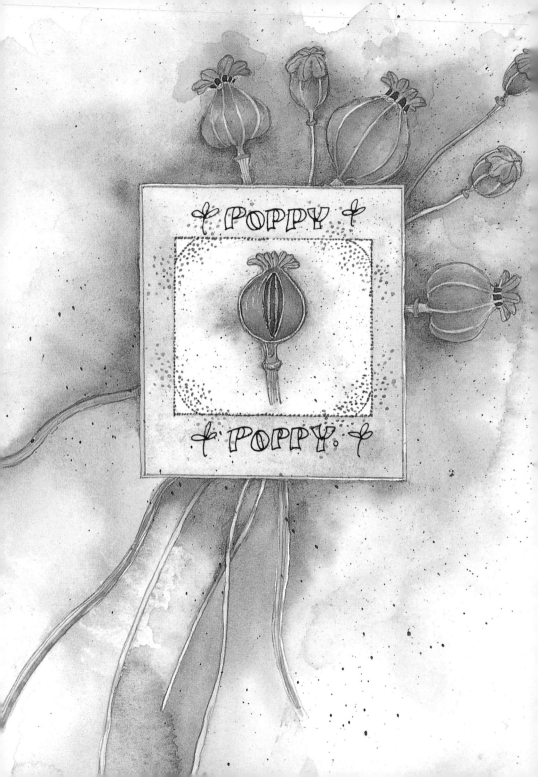

He who plants a garden, plants happiness.

CHINESE PROVERB

... a real gardener
is not a man who cultivates flowers;
he is a man who cultivates the soil.

KAREL CAPETE

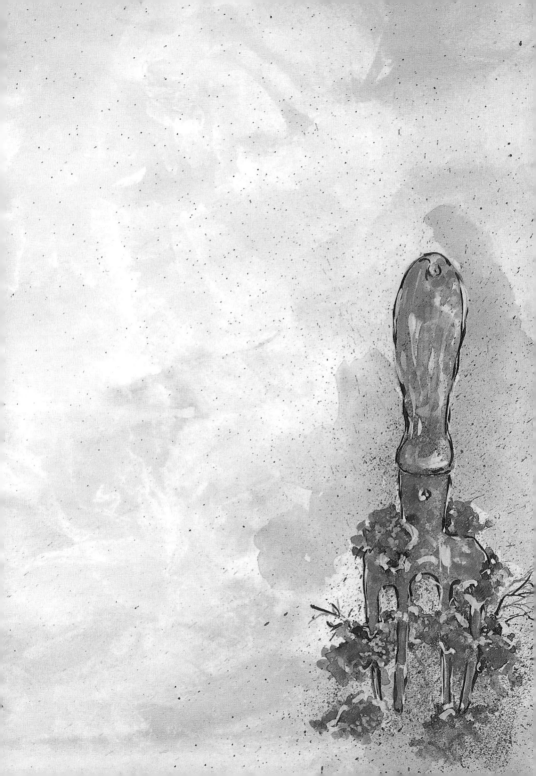

Probably more pests can be controlled
in an armchair in front of a February fire
with a garden notebook and a seed catalogue
than can ever be knocked out
in hand-to-hand combat in the garden.

NEELY TURNER

And why worry about clothes?
Look how the wild flowers grow:
they do not work or make clothes for themselves.
But I tell you that not even King Solomon
with all his wealth had clothes as beautiful
as one of these flowers.

FROM LUKE 16.13;28

GARDEN: One of a vast number of free outdoor restaurants operated by charity-minded amateurs in an effort to provide healthful, balanced meals for insects, birds, and animals.

HOSE: Crude, but effective and totally safe, type of scythe towed through gardens to flatten flower beds and level vegetable plantings.

PERENNIAL: Any plant which had it lived would have bloomed year after year.

HENRY BEARD AND ROY MCKIE,
FROM "GARDENING: A GARDENER'S DICTIONARY"

IF YOU TRULY LOVE NATURE,
YOU WILL FIND BEAUTY EVERYWHERE.

VINCENT VAN GOGH

Delphinium

Cranesbill

Forget-me-not

Pansy

Far beyond hope the Spring is kind again,
Lovely beyond the longing of my eyes.

MARGARET CROPPER

*There is one luxury item in the utilitarian garden:
a potting shed. I've just built one. It's a fabulous haven
among composts and flowerpots and forks.
As an escape from the family I recommend it with
no reservations at all!*

ALAN TITCHMARSH

You fight dandelions all weekend,
and late Monday afternoon
there they are, pert as all get out,
in full and gorgeous bloom,
pretty as can be,
thriving as only dandelions
can in the face of adversity.

HAL BORLAND

THE KISS OF THE SUN FOR PARDON,
THE SONG OF THE BIRDS FOR MIRTH,
ONE IS NEARER GOD'S HEART IN A GARDEN
THAN ANYWHERE ELSE ON EARTH.

DOROTHY FRANCES GURNEY

Earth laughs in flowers.

RALPH WALDO EMERSON

The daisy looks up in my face
As long ago it smiled.
It knows no change but keeps its place
And takes me for a child.

JOHN CLARE

In gardening, one's staunchest ally
is the natural lust for life each
plant has, that strong current which surges
through everything that grows.

JEAN HERSEY

A garden should be in a constant state of fluid change, expansion, experiment, adventure; above all it should be an inquisitive, loving but self-critical journey on the part of its owner.

H. E. BATES

One of the great things about gardening
is that when the huge wave of summer
does finally break, and its leaping curve
of green flings into every garden
a marvellous iridescent spray of petals,
in colours our language hasn't caught up with yet,
its joyful and indiscriminate tide lifts <u>everyone</u>
off their feet – both proper gardeners
and people like me.

PAUL JENNINGS

*B*eneath these fruit-tree boughs that shed
Their snow-white blossoms on my head,
With brightest sunshine round me spread
Of spring's unclouded weather,
In this sequestered nook how sweet
To sit upon my orchard-seat!
And birds and flowers once more to greet,
My last year's friends together.

WILLIAM WORDSWORTH, FROM "THE GREEN LINNET"

A GARDEN MAKES SURE
YOU ALWAYS HAVE SOMETHING TO WORRY ABOUT.

PAM BROWN

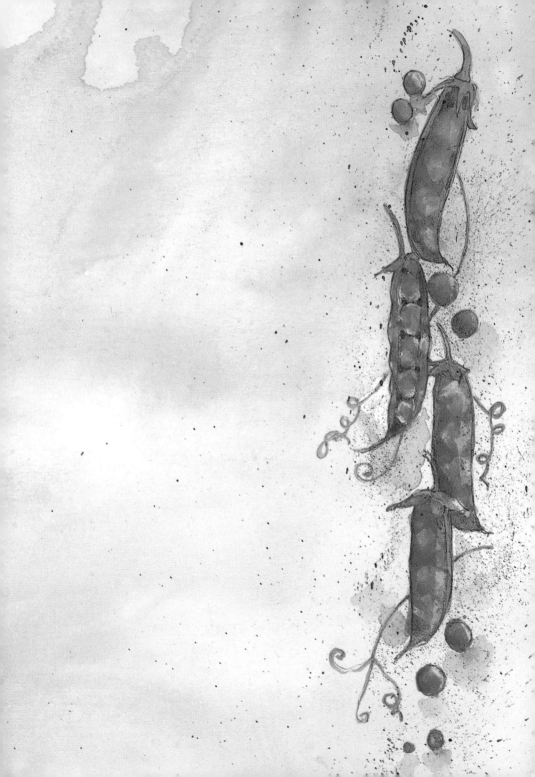

I should like to inflame

the whole world with my taste for gardens.

It seems to me impossible

for an evil-doer to share it.

PRINCE DE LIGNE

Gardening can become a kind disease. It infects you; you cannot escape it. When you go visiting, your eyes rove about the garden; you interrupt the serious cocktail drinking because of an irrestible impulse to get up and pull a weed.

LEWIS GANNIT

. nigella .

. . . love in the mist . . .

nigella . . . . nigella

love in the mist . . . Love in the mist . . . nigella

love in the mist .

. nigella . .

seeds

seeds from
inside the pod.

Love in the mist - nigella .

Juliette Clarke 1986

Mother's father had a touch
with horses; she had the same
with flowers. She could grow them
anywhere; at any time, and they seemed
to live longer for her.
She grew them with rough,
almost slap-dash love,
but her hands possessed
such an understanding
of their needs they seemed
to turn to her like another sun.

LAURIE LEE

Here's flowers for you;
Hot lavender, mints, savory, marjoram;
The marigold that goes to bed with the sun,
And with him rises weeping: these are flowers
Of middle summer, and I think they are given
To men of middle age.

WILLIAM SHAKESPEARE

*The work of a garden
bears visible fruits –
in a world where
most of our labours seem
suspiciously meaningless.*

PAM   BROWN

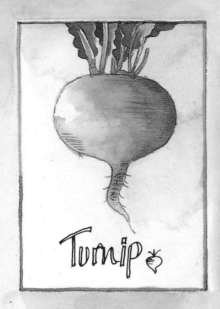

Turnip

Broad Bean

Peas

Onion

F<small>RUIT</small>: General term for the seed-bearing part of a plant that is eaten by birds or worms, drops off, rots, gets funny spots, isn't what was pictured in the catalogue, tastes like a glove or doesn't appear at all.

HENRY BEARD AND ROY MCKIE,
FROM "GARDENING: A GARDENER'S DICTIONARY"

For a person whose work
throws up an agreed set of figures
at the end of each day,
a garden is the last sane place on earth.

PAM BROWN

Those Latin Names

Who took me by the hand:
Why English flowers had Latin names
She couldn't understand,
Those funny, friendly English flowers,
That bloom from year to year –
She asked me if I would explain
And so I said to her:
Eranthis is an aconite
As everybody knows,
And Helleborous Niger is
Our friend the Christmas rose.
Galanthus is a snowdrop,
Matthiola is a stock,
And Cardamine the meadow flower
Which you call lady's smock.
Muscari is grape hyacinth.
Dianthus is a pink –
And that's as much as one small head
Can carry, I should think.
She listened, very patiently:
Then turned, when I had done,
To where a fine Forsythia
Was smiling in the sun.
Said she: "I <u>love</u> this yellow stuff".
And that, somehow, seemed praise enough.

REGINALD ARKELL

WHAT A MAN NEEDS IN GARDENING IS A CAST-IRON BACK
WITH A HINGE ON IT.

CHARLES DUDLEY WARNER

Home-made Jam

Apple Wine.

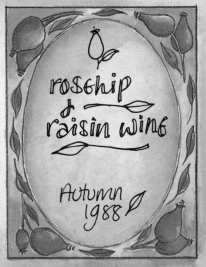

rosehip & raisin wine

Autumn 1988

Chamomile tea

I propose... to show, that, while, from a very small piece of ground,
a large part of the food of a considerable family may be raised,
the very act of raising it will be the best possible foundation of
<u>education</u> of the children of the labourer; that it will... give them the
best chance of leading happy lives.

WILLIAM COBBETT, FROM "COTTAGE ECONOMY"

Even if something is left undone,
everyone must take time to sit still
and watch the leaves turn.

ELIZABETH LAWRENCE

Look for a lovely thing and you will find it,
It is not far —
It will never be far.

SARA TEASDALE

GULP
I LOVED MY VEGETABLE GARDEN.
SO HERE IS MY SAD BALLAD:
I NURTURED IT FOR MONTHS
AND ATE IT IN ONE SALAD.

ARNOLD ZARETT

$\mathscr{A}$ garden is the purest of human pleasures.
It is the greatest refreshment to the spirits of man, without which
buildings and palaces are but gross handiworks.

FRANCIS BACON

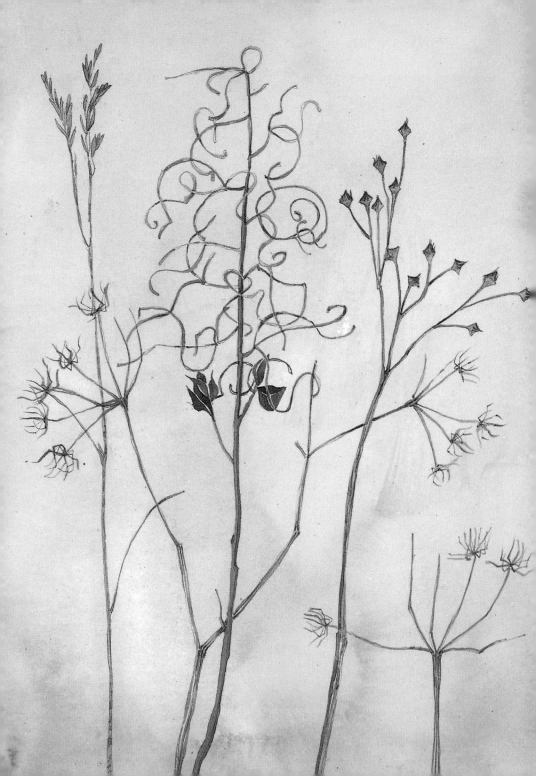

I believe a leaf of grass is no less than
the journey-work of the stars.

WALT WHITMAN

But a little garden,

the littler the better,

is your richest chance

for happiness and success.

REGINALD FARRER

* fennel *

· bay ·

· garlic ·

· sage ·

*The works of a person that builds
begin immediately to decay;
while those of him who plants
begin directly to improve.
In this, planting promises a
more lasting pleasure than building.*

WILLIAM SHENSTONE

Rockery: what the builder left behind.
Self-sufficiency gardening: a method of growing
vast supplies of the kinds of vegetables you would
never normally eat.
Soft fruit: bird sanctuary.

ROBIN CLARKE,
FROM "THE COMPLETELY UNILLUSTRATED ENCYCLOPAEDIA
OF GARDENING"

What is a weed?
A plant whose virtues have not yet been discovered.

RALPH WALDO EMERSON

BULB: potential flower buried in autumn,

never to be seen again.

CARROT: a special food grown for carrot flies.

DROUGHT: weather immediately following planting.

HOEING: manual method of severing roots from

stems of newly planted flowers and vegetables.

HENRY BEARD AND ROY MCKIE,
FROM "GARDENING: A GARDENER'S DICTIONARY"

*I don't know how people deal with their moods
when they have no garden, raspberry patch or field
to work in. You can take your angers, frustrations,
bewilderments to the earth, working savagely, working up
a sweat and an ache and a great weariness.
The work rinses out the cup of your spirit....*

RACHEL PEDEN

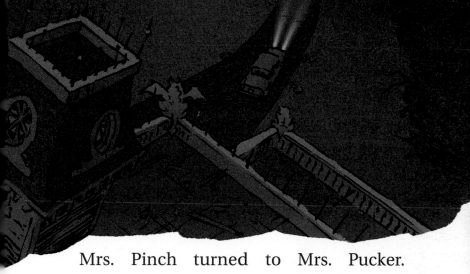

Mrs. Pinch turned to Mrs. Pucker. "There's something very strange going on in Old Howl Hall," she said. "I had better tell Lester to keep his eye on those Howls."

"I told you," said Mrs. Pucker, puckering her lips. "I told you that place was creepy!"

"Well, for once you may be right," said Mrs. Pinch.

"What a bunch of party poopers," said Mrs. Plum. "*I* had a great time!"

After the car had disappeared down the driveway, Jack Howl walked into the dining room.

"Dad," said Axel. "You missed every-thing!"

"Yeah!" said Thistle. "There was the most amazing silver wolf! It came right into our house."

"I wonder where it went?" said Axel.

Jack winked at Wanda.

"I wish that wolf would come back," said Thistle with a sigh.

"Me too," said Axel.

"Perhaps one day the wolf will come back," said Jack Howl with a secret smile. "You never know...."